RIGHT OPPORTUNITY IN WRONG TIME

YOU ARE ENOUGH TO TAKE BOLD DECISION

SANTA SUNIL KUMAR

ISBN 979-888555665-1

TO LOVERS OF BOOKS...........

I AM SO HAPPY THAT YOU GAVE LIFE TO THIS BOOK THROUGH READING.

THIS BOOK IS DEDICATED TO ALL OF YOU ESPECIALLY ASPIRANTS WHO DARE TO DREAM

The WINGS OF THIS BOOK COMES FROM FAMILY, FRIENDS AND CLOSE RELATIV

Contents

Foreword

We got this book last month while one of our students was having a hard time. We recommended this book to him. He called us after two days to share his experience. "Problems are common, but solutions are always unique," he said. Yes, this book will help you find solutions to problems and also understand the most important thing in our lives: that problems are common for all.

FROM,

DR SHINE V.J AND DR ANUJA SHINA

Preface

If success is not the result of pain and suffering, then the entire country of India may be able to realize their aspirations in a very short period of time. THEN OUR LIVES APPEAR TO BE MECHANICAL, DON'T THEY? LIFE BECOMES INTERESTING WHEN WE HAVE BIG GOALS TO ACHIEVE, JUST LIKE IN THIS BOOK'S GIRL'S LIFE. DREAMS WILL COME TRUE FOR ALL THOSE WHO ARE WILLING TO DREAM BIGGER THAN THEIR LIMIT.

She struggled a lot on her way from being a rural, middle-class girl to an IAS officer. One of her favourite books as a child was I Am Malala: The Girl Who Stood Up For Education And Was Shot By The TALIBAN. Mala desired a good height, but God placed her in the highest position later—this line inspired her a lot.

Preface

If success is not the result of pain and suffering, then the entire country of India may be able to realize their aspirations in a very short period of time. THEN OUR LIVES APPEAR TO BE MECHANICAL, DON'T THEY? LIFE BECOMES INTERESTING WHEN WE HAVE BIG GOALS TO ACHIEVE, JUST LIKE IN THIS BOOK'S GIRL'S LIFE. DREAMS WILL COME TRUE FOR ALL THOSE WHO ARE WILLING TO [illegible] BIGGER THAN THEIR [illegible]

She struggled a lot on her way from being a rural middle-class girl to an [illegible]. One of her favourite books as a child was I Am Malala: The Girl Who Stood Up for Education and Was Shot By The TALIBAN. Malala deserved a good height, but God placed her in the [illegible] [illegible]—this unreasonable [illegible].

Acknowledgements

This page is extremely important for a beginning writer. The most difficult problem a writer may face in completing a book is a lack of inspiration. Miracles Happen Through Books if She or He Is Filled With Happiness. I avail myself this opportunity to express my sincere gratitude to inspiration fillers .....

Thank you, especially to God, for showing me that little flower from whom I was inspired to write her life.

Thank you my dear family for your faith in me.

THANK YOU FOR PUBLISHING MY DREAMS, NOTION PRESS......

Thank you, dear readers, for making my dream come true.

Inspired Quote

" "GOD HAS PREPARED A PATH FOR EVERYONE TO FOLLOW"
----- THE ALCHEMIST
------ PAULO COELHO"

Prologue

I KNOW SOME PEOPLE WORK HARD TO FOLLOW THEIR DREAM. ONE OF THEM WAS ME. I DON'T KNOW THE EXACT DATE OR TIME WHEN I SHARE MY DREAM OF BECOMING A CIVIL SERVANT WITH MY FAMILY. BUT THAT DAY CHANGED MY LIFE DRASTICALLY. AFTER THAT, IT WAS NOT AT ALL EASY. NEWSPAPER, NCERT, AND STANDARD BOOKS APPEAR TO BE MAKING ME A CRAZY PERSON. THERE WERE TIMES WHEN I DID NOT HAVE TIME TO PREPARE. BUT I MANAGED TO OVERCOME.

This is, indeed, my tale.

SANCHA KUMAR

IAS

2002

Right Opportunity In Wrong Time

HERE WE BEGIN...

CHAPTER ONE

DAY OF MEMORIES

Cheers from the audience for India. The culmination of Indian dreams occurred on April 2nd, 2011. I recall that special day when the most beautiful moment in all of our hearts was born: "World Cup 2011." From 2011 to 2022—it seems like it was only yesterday. I was only nine years old. There was no television to witness that wonderful moment. My mother and I dashed towards our neighbors' house with my heart racing. I'm not sure what time it was. In any case, it's the middle of the night. Tension held my small hands in prayer position, hoping for miracles from God. All prayers will, indeed, be answered. With a single ball from a great legend's bat touching the doors of the silent sky "M.S DHONI," dreams became a reality. I'll remember 2011 for one more thing: MASTER BLASTER SACHIN TENDULKAR's final world cup. Those were fleeting moments. However, it had a significant impact on my limited intellect. At the eleventh hour, I began to believe in miracles. Whether you're having trouble or not, the perfect remedy will arrive at the right time, just like Mahi Bhaiya's batting. In the future, I wanted to be a cracker, I DECIDED.

I was born and raised in one of India's most beautiful states. My state stood out because of its beautiful scenery, festivals, and traditions. For the first time, Kerala, "God's own country," told me I was special. I'd heard a lot about her when I was a kid.

KERALA BEAUTY

HOUSE BOAT

.During my childhood, I used to build air castles in order to become a cricketer who could perform feats of magic with his bat. If you had asked that little girl twenty-one years ago, "Dear, Please tell me one thing that makes you happier. She'll say anything with her enthusiastic eyes, but not I.A.S. But don't anticipate the same response from me right now. I.A.S. is my breath today, and I can't leave without it. The road to I.A.S. taught me who I am. I.A.S. I once prayed to be able to wear a T-shirt bearing Indian name. Through my vocation, God has made me bear the same name in my heart today. God, thank you.

CHAPTER TWO

MESSAGE FROM PAST TO FUTURE

"One day, everyone will listen to me, and then I will start speaking for my country"

These phrases have a unique meaning for me since they reflect my inner turmoil.

These are some lines from an old diary of mine (sixth standard). That particular day was not particularly pleasant for me. But today it is different because that day instilled courage in me. I was short and didn't have enough height to keep my spirits up. I don't recall the episode, but I'm certain, it had something to do with my height and weight. When I was little, I used to be taller than my peers. But back then, I used to resent God for giving me more height than my peers. My height became my adversary, forcing me to take a step back.

I'd like to take the lead and represent my class, but nothing seems to work. Friends, a little request: never blame God for your circumstances. It may appear insignificant to your eyes, yet it is priceless to others. I regret what I did after many years, and I am confident that God will hear me.

My desire to become taller kept me up at night. YouTube videos on healthy nutrition and exercise, among other things, drove me insane. However, poetry was one thing that helped me avoid unpleasant days. I was given the opportunity to compete in a poetry competition. The theme was "There is Something Beyond Every Mountain". Yes, there is a solution to every issue. To achieve that goal, one must strive to eliminate negativity. I owe a debt of gratitude to my college's dean.

Beyond every mountain, there is something special.
I lifted my brows.
A new world is on the horizon.
They drew me back.
I will do so one day.
My shell must be broken.

CHAPTER THREE

LESSONS TO LEARN

School days, like those of any other person, are always memorable for me. The best thing about school days was that we weren't permitted to use our phones, even on school trips. So, via my eyes, I was able to preserve those lovely memories that are impervious to tear and wear. I'm sorry, but the person reading this book may not be able to connect with me. Our phones have been our best friends in recent years. Consider a time when you forgot to bring your phone with you. You'll feel unfinished or uninterested. We are now evolving toward a virtual world in which you can communicate with anyone without any barriers. I recall a time when Facebook and Instagram stopped working.

...I'm sure that day was the happiest day in the lives of many families.

The only way to envisage a bright future is via education. What I am now is solely due to the hardships I experienced during my school years. I owe my parents gratitude for allowing me to soar without enclosing me in a golden cage. In our lives, everything is connected. When difficulties arise, always be prepared to work hard even in the midst of a raging sea. Because the raging water will put your courage to the test, you will be able to sail further to your success. As a result, success is always the result of suffering and hard work. Try to appreciate the little things in life. If you're fatigued or frustrated, take a step back and look at the bigger picture.

Being impoverished does not imply that you are unhappy.

My parents, brother, grandparents, uncle, aunt, and sisters created a little heaven in my family. I used to despise two things in school. The first is the day of the exam results. Exams are simple to write because you use all of your talents to present your answers and keep repeating, "I'm going to rock." However, the day of the exam result announcement is not one to be taken lightly. After many days, you realized that your expectations were wrong on that day. I used to hide my grades from the rest of the class, and the rest of the time I preferred to assist a friend who did well in class in determining where she missed one mark. After many years, I passed India's most challenging and prestigious examination, the UPSC. Thank you, God. And this is my message to all of you, quantitative parameters like marks are nothing in life's success.

CHAPTER FOUR

CHOICES MAKES THE DIFFERENCE

Options * VARY FROM PERSON TO PERSON, AND WHAT YOU LIKE MAY NOT BE MY FAVORITE. VARY FROM PERSON TO PERSON, AND WHAT YOU LIKE MAY NOT BE MY FAVORITE. One of my favorite poem is POSSIBILITY by WISLAAWA

"Wislaawa" was my inspiration for writing this story.

POSSIBILITIES SUMMARY

I PREFER THE FRONT PAGES OF NEWSPAPERS TO GRIMMS' FAIRY TALE "

NON - SPECIFIC ANNIVERSARIES ARE MY FAVOURITE"

(IF U GET A CHANCE TO READ THIS POEM, PLEASE READ)

There is no choice to dream, choose a career, or believe in one's own hard work. Don't blame it on the fact that you're poor. One of the reasons is poverty, but the main reason is fear. Opinions are the source of fear. India is the most important market for views that turn out to be facts. The only thing you can receive without spending money is a viewpoint. It will begin during the school days. From the poorest high school to the greatest. Everything is publicly available, from the lowest to the greatest conceivable score, from the worst comparison to the finest. All you need is a good pair of ears to hear them. Now tell me whether or not our country values variety. In many ways, our country fails to grasp the genuine spirit of choices when half of the population has no say in their destiny. My relatives, friends, and even strangers gave me excellent advice when I decided to seek a career as a Civil Servant.

But I wasn't prepared to return. I, too, chose a different route than Robert Frost (that a middle-class aspirant would not dare to do).

Two roads diverged into a yellow wood, and I'm sorry, I could not travel both. I took the less-traveled route, and it made all the difference.

CHOICES IN OUR LIFE

It was such a lovely poem, that motivated me to conquer my difficulties. I hope this poem will assist you in overcoming your challenges and achieving your objectives as quickly as possible.

CHAPTER FIVE

HAPPINESS

NEVER SEARCH FOR HAPPINESS, CREATE IT

This world is never exactly what it appears to be. When I left the four walls of my high school and college, I witnessed a world of difference. My thoughts had gone blank. I was drawn to it by a well-known question. What's next? To acquire a career, I chose to study for state competitive tests. People saw me carrying a massive rank file at all hours of the day and night. Nothing, however, worked. I was one of the 55% of individuals in the middle-class family who never chose to take chances. All of my examinations were a failure. I'd failed again. But it was then that I realized the actual meaning of life. However, rather than seeking temporal fulfillment, one should seek pleasure. When you strive to wall yourself away from happiness, you will not find it. When you try to trap yourself in something you don't enjoy for the sake of someone else's pleasure, happiness will not come to you. Will fame and fortune bring you happiness? Did you feel fulfilled after accomplishing a goal for someone else? Make an effort to make yourself joyful at all times. Our own lives can serve as a simple illustration. Consider a day when you are depressed and everything seems to be going wrong. You will become enraged about minor issues, or you may spend your entire day worrying about them. The finest present you can offer yourself is happiness. I'm sure you've heard of Leo Tolstoy's renowned novel "DEATH OF IVAN ILYCH"

This book will assist you in distinguishing between a worthwhile life and a pointless, money-oriented existence. Ivan was a gifted student when he was a youngster. He ascended the corporate ladders by separating his work achievements from his unpleasant personal life. However, a minor mishap taught him the value of living a decent life. But it was too late to correct his error. In a nutshell, I'm trying to suggest that you should always attempt to do what you enjoy. Money is nothing if you don't live a tranquil life.

How Do You Find Happiness?

• Set a goal that makes you happy.

• Don't think about the past or the future, which you can't change.

• Make an effort to be grateful for the little things in life.

1. BE UNIQUE—NEVER COMPARE YOURSELF WITH OTHERS
2. TRUST IN YOU WHEN WORLD SAY YOU CAN'T MOVE
3. SPREAD HAPPINESS TO OTHERS
4. ALWAYS PRAY

HAPPINESS ALL WE NEED

CHAPTER SIX

OK TO BE IMPERFECT

We strive to be flawless in all we do, from our personal lives to our professional lives. However, striving for perfection will leave you unsatisfied with all you have accomplished. When I initially started my civil service career, the first answer I practiced was the worst answer I'd ever written. But that didn't bother me. And it was because of that flaw that I was able to achieve this accomplishment. Do you know why people are afraid of being flawed? The basic answer is that I am concerned about what others may think of me. They may make fun of me if I don't get a good grade." HOW OLD ARE YOU?" was a Malayalam film that I recall seeing. This is a basic illustration of how fear enslaves our dreams and how to conquer them. When the key character of this film meets the "PRESIDENT OF INDIA," she becomes unconscious. She, on the other hand, was not ready to settle down. She got it back to her starting spot from her lowest moment and saw the same person after achieving her goal in life. I strongly suggest you see that video whenever you have the chance; it will motivate you to take action.

PERFECTLY
IMPERFECT

CHAPTER SEVEN

KERALA IN SHORT

SADYA -- ONAM FEAST

VALLAM KALI -- TRADITIONAL BOAT RACE IN KERALA

ELEPHANT ---STATE ANIMAL OF KERALA

Sree Padmanabha Swamy Temple,
Thiruvananthapuram, Kerala, India

RICE FIELD

Theyyam is a ritual form in Kerala, India. This particular Theyyam is one variation of 'Pottan Theyyam', a vivid, lively and colorful ritualistic performance that comes in the traditional art form of Theyyam.

HAPPY CHILD COLLECTING FLOWERS FOR MAKING ONAM POOKALAM Onam festival is celebrated to honor the kind-hearted and much-beloved demon King

Mahabali, who is believed to return to Kerala during this festival.

Santa Cruz Cathedral Basilica Fort Kochi

JATAYU PARK IN KOLLAM

Athirappilly Falls is situated in Athirappilly Panchayat in Chalakudy Taluk of Thrissur

Positivity

HOW ARE YOU? People have a propensity of starting discussions with a negative tone. YOU APPEAR TIRED BY THE BY. WHY DO YOU APPEAR TO BE SO DULL? I HAD HEARD ABOUT YOUR EXAM FAILURE. DO YOU KNOW NEENA? SHE DID WELL IN SECONDARY SCHOOL, BUT HOW ABOUT YOU? In your daily life, you can run across a lot of these types of queries. But you have no idea how much of an influence it will have. It's enough to ruin the rest of the day. Let's pretend we're in a circumstance where we'll run across an old pal. You started off on the wrong foot with your talk.

MAHA, HAI I HEARD THE PANDEMIC AFFECTED YOU SO BADLY THAT YOU LOST YOUR JOB, ISN'T IT?

If Maha replies badly, as you upset her at the introduction itself, it will be the end of a beautiful friendship.

Remember that the mind is like a wooden board. When you are furious, you strike an iron rod into it, and when you are calm, you remove it. However, the wooden board is no longer as robust.

Take care with your remarks. Your words have the power to shape or destroy people.

So, always maintain positivity around you...............................

Will Continue

THANK YOU

9 798885 556651

Printed by Libri Plureos GmbH in Hamburg, Germany